Source of Life
The Eucharist and Christian Living

Source of Life

The Eucharist and Christian Living

RENÉ VOILLAUME
translated by
DINAH LIVINGSTONE

LIVING FLAME PRESS
LOCUST VALLEY, N.Y. 11560

First published as
Ma Chair Pour La Vie du Monde
by Editions due Cerf, Paris
This translation first published in England
in 1975 and copyrighted by
Darton, Longman and Todd, Ltd., 1975

U.S. edition published by Living Flame Press
Locust Valley, N.Y. 11560

ISBN 0-232-51298-1

Printed in the United States of America

Contents

The Eucharist as Fact and Historical Reality

I am a little nervous about giving a talk on Christ and the Eucharist. It is such an important subject for christians and such a difficult one, although it also has a divine simplicity.

In the first place, the Eucharist, the body of Christ, the cup of Christ's blood, the holy bread, the blessed sacrament is a reality, a fact. It has belonged to mankind since a certain historical moment and to the church from its beginning. We have the Eucharist, we cannot get rid of it, if I may put it that way, it is with us till Christ returns. It is a mystery, a mystery of faith, which there has been a lot of argument about. There is a famous fresco in the Vatican, by Michelangelo, I think, which is called "The Dispute over the Holy Sacrament". Around it stand the most intelligent men from every age, discussing, meditating or looking shocked. They are talking about the mystery.

All the christian churches have the Eucharist. And so we have to keep asking: what is this bread and this

consecrated wine? Some are shocked by it. They want
to understand it by reason, to diminish or spiritualize
this presence. Others are over-realistic about Jesus'
physical presence. They try to imagine how it could be
Christ enclosed in the bread! "The prisoner in the
tabernacle"! Feelings also become involved. There
have been periods of intense sentimental piety based
on a false notion of Christ's presence.

But is the scandal of the Eucharist any worse than
the scandal of Jesus himself? Now the Eucharist is a
problem to us, but we must not forget that for rather
more than thirty years a man walked on earth among
us who caused even greater scandal and disquiet to
his fellows. Christ is no longer present in this way on
earth. He is in the glory of his Father and for the last
two thousand years christians have been trying to live
by faith in him and to act with the love which he sowed
in human hearts. During this time Christ has been far
above in his glory and perhaps no longer scandalizes
us.

But let us try to imagine what it was like for Israel
and the most enlightened Jews of that time. They were
confronted with the extraordinary phenomenon of a
man going about among their people calling himself
the Messiah and the Son of God. The Messiah was
expected, he was to re-establish the kingdom of Israel.

But this is not what Jesus did. From his birth onwards he met extraordinary antagonism. People were afraid of him. A sovereign prince wanted to eliminate him the moment he was born, because he was afraid and distrusted him. After this Jesus lived in obscurity for nearly thirty years. He was a man like others, a village tradesman, living in Nazareth which had a bad reputation and which at that time was a much less important township than it is now. When he came into the open, people neither understood nor believed.

Jesus was not understood even by his own people, particularly at Nazareth. They knew him too well. Was not this the village carpenter? Where did he get this knowledge? His own people did not accept him; his family, his cousins did not believe in him. Why should they have? He had not studied, he was not a priest, he was not of the tribe of Levi and could not enter the sanctuary of the Temple. Who was this man? The Pharisees did not believe in him. Jerusalem did not believe. That is why he wept over Jerusalem. At first even the apostles did not believe in his resurrection, they needed time to accept it. People disbelieved and they also accused him. He was accused of being a drunkard, a soak, the friend of publicans and sinners, possessed by the devil, a Samaritan, a madman. They said : he is a sinner, he breaks the sabbath; what right has he to do what he does and speak as he speaks? He witnesses against himself, he cannot come from God because he breaks the sabbath. Then they accused him of stirring up the people, spreading disorder and blaspheming. He blasphemed by forgiving sins, and by calling himself God's equal. He called himself the son of God, he was an impostor! He called himself Christ the king, so he was Caesar's enemy! What a lot of noise – God alone knew how many simple and upright hearts accepted his word and profited by it.

Why should the Eucharist which is now, and always will be among us, be better understood than Christ himself? People saw Jesus as just a man, a poor and ordinary citizen of Nazareth. That is why it was so hard to believe in him. The Eucharist is, after all, just bread. It would be so much easier to see it as merely a symbol. It would be so reasonable. It would be so much easier to see the consecrated wine as the sign of Jesus' blood, a simple memorial.

Such is the fact of the Eucharist. This is why it is at the heart of the church, the christian faith and our relationship with Christ. We cannot go to Jesus if we disregard the Eucharist, it is not possible. So it is very important to understand, if possible as Jesus himself understood, what the Eucharist is.

That is why I am going to talk first about the

Eucharist in the mind of Christ, in the light of the gospel and the faith of the church. Then we will talk about how we should behave towards the Eucharist, what our response should be to this gift Christ has given us.

The Eucharist, Christ's Creation

Is it possible for us to find out what Jesus thought about it? For he is the first person we ought to ask. I do not think we can penetrate the mystery of the Eucharist without first considering the incarnation, that mysterious union between the created world and the eternal God the creator. I was going to call it that union between two extremes, God, of whom the Jews had a very elevated and pure conception after centuries of divine instruction, God eternal, invisible, transcendent, almighty, the creator of all things, whom no man can see and live; and man, such a humble being, and so many of us.

We do not even understand ourselves. We know that we have a heart and mind. We know that our heart and mind work through our senses, our bodies. We are mysterious, part spirit, part flesh, with death and decay at our end. We have no experience of glory, yet for most men it means nothing. We have no experience of life as a pure spirit, and that is why we con-

tinually fall back on materialism. The weight of our
flesh, the weight of our senses, the weight even of our
knowledge, always brings us back to matter, to a more
and more complex matter. That is why our spiritual
side tends to get lost.

The incarnation bridges the gulf between man and
this supreme being, about whom we would know
nothing if he had not revealed something of his inner
life. God's eternal word became flesh, became Jesus.
He was born and he also died. He came to give life
and he came to reveal the Father. He is the image of
the Father. He is the word; faith feeds our minds, and
the word feeds this faith; so Jesus chose bread. The
greatest mysteries often lie in the simplest things. Jesus
was born in Bethlehem, the house of bread, if we trans-
late the Hebrew. But when Jesus quietly left his house
and Nazareth his home and went into the wilderness to
face his future, his saviourhood, the coming cross and
passion, the three years of teaching which were to end
on Calvary, he was tempted. He was hungry. The
tempter tried to persuade him to turn stones into bread.
Jesus answered, "It is written, man shall not live by
bread alone but by every word that comes from the
mouth of God."[1] Jesus *is* this word; he will feed us.
Later Jesus enjoyed multiplying the loaves, not once

[1] Mt. 4.4.

but twice. These were his two great miracles which caused the greatest stir. After one of them the people wanted to carry him off and make him king. As they saw it, it was very useful for a leader to be able to feed the poor and hungry simply by his will. He could give bread whenever they wanted. It seems likely that when Jesus multiplied the loaves he was also thinking of that other multiplication of bread, the consecration of the Eucharist throughout the centuries. He also multiplied the fishes. Fish was to become a sign of Jesus among the early christians because the letters of the Greek word fish were the initials of his title.[2] The bread was multiplied indefinitely and lost none of its power to feed the individual.

After the resurrection the disciples met Christ again, in the flesh but risen, his glory still concealed, so that they did not even recognize him. They recognized Jesus because he sat at table with them, took bread, blessed and broke it and gave it to them. Their eyes were opened and they recognized him because he had given them the bread.

There is a close, even natural, connection between the divine word feeding our minds and Christ's body feeding the life of the spirit. It belongs to the logic of the incarnation. Our spirits are in the flesh. Our

[2] *ichthus*: Jesus Christ, son of God, Saviour.

creator knows what we are better than we know ourselves. The word of God given through the prophets,
given by the Son himself, feeds our minds and becomes
our spiritual bread. That is why Jesus is bread in the
most spiritual sense of the word. But how can he feed
the human mind with more than a knowledge which
is dead and abstract, how can this knowledge become
life and love and transform us into the likeness of the
Son of God? We cannot do it by ourselves, we are too
weak. We need food which can reach our innermost
being, to cure, redeem and strengthen us, to enable us
to put God's word into practice. So Jesus gave himself
to be our food, not just spiritually, but truly, in his body,
in his humanity.

The Eucharist expresses admirably the bond between
God and us which is the end of the incarnation's
purpose. The Eucharist is the sign best suited to make
us understand its real meaning.

*

Now we must try and listen to what Jesus tried to
tell us in the central discourse of St John's gospel, on
the bread of life. This discourse was a climax in the
preaching of Jesus, and extraordinarily bold and clear.
Jesus has just worked the miracle of the loaves and

because of this the crowds are following him. "Truly, truly, I say to you, you seek me, not because you saw signs, but because you ate your fill of the loaves. Do not labour for the food which perishes, but for the food which endures to eternal life, which the Son of man will give to you; for on him has God the Father set his seal."[3]

Then when the people mention Moses who gave the people manna in the wilderness he says: "Truly, truly, I say to you, it was not Moses who gave you the bread from heaven; my Father gives you the true bread from heaven. For the bread of God is that which comes down from heaven, and gives life to the world."[4]

This bread is Jesus. By his incarnation Jesus was given like bread which gives life to the world. The Father gives us him, the whole Jesus, Jesus with his teaching and the grace he has which he passes on to all the members of his mystical body. Then the crowd, which still does not understand, says to him, "Lord give us this bread always."[5]

This is like what the Samaritan woman said at Jacob's well, "Sir, give me this water, that I may not thirst, nor come here to draw."[6]

[3] Jn. 6.26–7.
[4] Jn. 6.32–3.
[5] Jn. 6.34.
[6] Jn. 4.15.

We would so like to be able to change our short, painful and limited lives into eternal life. And Jesus answers them : "I am the bread of life; he who comes to me shall not hunger, and he who believes in me shall never thirst. But I said to you that you have seen me and yet do not believe."[7]

He asks them to have faith. I am here, you see me, but you do not believe." These words of Jesus fell on dull hearts, closed minds, gross spirits only looking for immediate satisfactions.

This provokes Jesus to go even further. The Father gave us Jesus who is the bread of life and now Jesus gives himself to us in the Eucharist : "I am the living bread which came down from heaven; if anyone eats of this bread, he will live for ever."[8]

Jesus is bread. The bread is a symbol of Jesus who is the food of eternal life – through all that he is, through his teaching, through his word, because he is the word of God, source of life and forgiveness of sins. Jesus adds : "And the bread which I shall give for the life of the world is my flesh." This time it is not the Father who is the life-giver. Jesus gives himself in his human nature to be our food. This is the first time Jesus has spoken openly, and as we shall see, in such a matter-of-

[7] Jn. 6 : 35.
[8] Jn. 6.51.

fact way, of the Eucharist. None of them can understand him, not even his apostles, let alone this crowd who came after him for bread. Jesus speaks for all generations to come, because he cannot be understood until after his passion. "And the bread which I shall give for the life of the world is my flesh." The Jews protest: "How can this man give us his flesh to eat?" Jesus does not explain but insists: "Truly, truly I say to you, unless you eat the flesh of the Son of Man and drink his blood, you have no life in you; he who eats my flesh and drinks my blood has eternal life, and I will raise him up at the last day. For my flesh is food indeed and my blood is drink indeed." He really rubs it in as if he *wanted* to shock them. They say: "This is a hard saying; who can listen to it?"[9]

They are simple people, they are not only wondering how a living man can give his flesh to eat and his blood to drink, but for Jews such a claim was also irreligious. In the Law and all their tradition it was strictly forbidden to drink blood. For the blood contained the life force and they were forbidden to touch it. "You shall eat no blood whatever . . . in any of your dwellings. Whoever eats any blood, that person shall be cut off from his people." And again: "No person among you shall eat blood . . . for the life of every creature is the

[9] Jn. 6.51–60.

blood of it; therefore I have said to the people of Israel, You shall not eat the blood of any creature, for the life of every creature is its blood; whoever eats it shall be cut off."[10] Jesus is wilfully scandalizing them by saying: "You will drink my blood, my blood is drink indeed." It is natural that they should react with "This is a hard saying; who can listen to it?" And so they leave him.

What is Jesus' answer? He explains nothing away. He merely says: "Do you take offence at this? Then what if you were to see the Son of Man ascending where he was before?" Nothing else. A great mystery has been revealed. He continues: "It is the spirit that gives life, the flesh is of no avail." There is nothing more to say. "After this," says the evangelist, "many of his disciples drew back and no longer went about with him." It was too much. We cannot set aside this discourse of Jesus, because it is what he himself taught. His words were clear, plain enough to shock his disciples, Jesus let them go and retracted nothing. Without any further explanation he merely said to the twelve: "Will you also go away?" And Peter answered: "Lord, to whom shall we go? You have the words of eternal life."[11]

He didn't understand either, perhaps he was also

[10] Lev. 7.26–7; 17.12, 14.
[11] Jn. 6.61–2, 66–8.

shocked, but he did not want to leave Jesus. Who could he go to? I think that we all too are shocked by the Eucharist. If we are, Jesus merely says: "Will you also go away?" I do not see how it would be possible to make sense of this if the Eucharist was nothing but a memorial, a symbol of the Lord, and if in it we did not truly receive his humanity.

We can neither get rid of the mystery of the Eucharist nor stop it puzzling us. Since the last supper, from generation to generation, from consecration to consecration, the bread and the cup of the blood has been shared among us. We cannot stop it happening, indeed we cannot! The Eucharist is with us, it has become part of humanity.

It is a mystery of faith. And because there is a close connection between blood, which the Jews thought of as the principle of life and the purpose for which Jesus wished to give us his blood to drink, it means that Jesus wanted to give us himself as the very principle of our life, our new and eternal life.

*

We have to read the story of the institution of the Eucharist in the light of these words of Jesus. We have to suspend our reason, if that is not too bold a way of putting it, and come to the story with childlike faith. We are at the heart of the kingdom of God and Jesus told us that if we did not become as little children we could not enter the kingdom of God. Of course we can and should give our minds to the mystery. But can we understand it? We have to know what we ought to believe, and that must surely be the words of Jesus himself.

We see the mystery as the supreme sign of Jesus' love, that is the first thing. "Greater love has no man than this, that a man lay down his life for his friends."[12]

It is the eve of Jesus' death. "I have earnestly desired to eat this passover with you before I suffer; for I tell you I shall not eat it again until it is fulfilled in the kingdom of God."[13]

This is the climax of the incarnation. Jesus is about to suffer and then it will all be over. He will no longer be with us, he will not share bread and wine with us again until the kingdom of God comes – "until he comes"[14] says St Paul, until he comes!

"This is my beloved Son; listen to him."[15]

[12] Jn. 15.13.
[13] Lk. 22.15.
[14] I Cor. 11.26.
[15] Mk. 9.7.

Yesterday[16] we were reminded that the transfiguration of Jesus was a sort of parenthesis interrupting the scandal he aroused by what he was and did, a parenthesis which only two or three special friends were privileged to experience.

It was like a lightning flash suddenly illuminating the glory of the Son of God hidden in the Son of Man. And it was then that God the Father commanded us to listen to him.

"Jesus took bread, and blessed, and broke it, and gave it to the disciples and said, 'Take, eat; this is my body.' And he took a cup, and when he had given thanks he gave it to them, saying, 'Drink of it, all of you; for this is my blood of the covenant, which is poured out for many for the forgiveness of sins.' "[17]

Jesus said : "This is my body." The apostles and the first christians received this mysterious institution of the Eucharist from Christ himself and they repeated it because he said : "Do this in memory of me." St Paul also tells us : "For I received from the Lord what I also delivered to you."[18]

He received it from the apostles who had seen the Lord. He received it from Peter and John and James,

[16] August 6, the feast of the Transfiguration always solemnly celebrated at Taizé.
[17] Mt. 26.26–8.
[18] 1 Cor. 11.23.

and Paul repeats the story we quoted above almost word for word, the story set down by the apostles in the gospel. Then he adds: "For as often as you eat this bread and drink the cup, you proclaim the Lord's death until he comes."[19]

That is all. He gives no further explanation or commentary. We may well ask what the apostles made of all that was improbable, mysterious, of the factual content of the institution they had received at the Last Supper and repeated after the death, resurrection and ascension of Jesus.

After giving the testimony of St Paul, we may also quote here a text of St Cyril which Paul VI used in his encyclical *Mysterium Fidei*.[20]

"This is my body which is given for you", writes St Cyril and goes on to say, "Do not wonder whether it is true but receive the words of the Lord with faith, because he who is truth does not lie." Jesus is not only Truth, but he also has the power to make what he says come true because he is the Word. All things were made by him and without him nothing was made that was made. "This is my body." This means it is really the body of Christ. "This is my blood" – really the blood of Christ. This makes it all the more important to remem-

19 1 Cor. 11.26.
20 Mysterium Fidei, 18.

ber the teaching of Jesus in his discourse on the bread of life, in which he spoke of his flesh as food indeed and his blood as drink indeed and thoroughly shocked his disciples.

In all the marvellously various liturgies of the Eucharist the bread is always consecrated by priests or ministers who repeat the Lord's own words, because they must be repeated and not altered and Jesus said : "Do this in memory of me."

In the ancient coptic liturgy which goes back to the desert fathers and has kept its primitive simplicity, the words of consecration of the bread and wine are interrupted by the acclamations of the people : "Amen this is the truth, we believe it." This is repeated after almost each word of consecration. It's true, we believe it. That is all. What is there to add?

*

This is why we believe that Jesus' presence in the Eucharist is a true and real presence. Why should we be shocked? It is less difficult for the divine omnipotence to assume such a presence than for the Word to become flesh and be made man. Jesus gave us the Eucharist and he was fully able to do so. In the faith of the church and the faith of the gospel the bread changed into his body and the wine into his blood have of course a close connection with his passion and are a memorial of the Lord's death, the covenant in his blood. It is necessary that this covenant should be continued till the end of the church on earth because it must be able to reach all men, this offering for the forgiveness of sins was "for many", as Jesus himself said.

It must be able to reach all human generations. That is why the Word became flesh and Jesus died. The mystery had to be released from temporal limitations and available to every believer who wanted to come close to Christ, to be purified by him, transfigured and given new life and the pledge of future glory and resurrection.

It would be wrong to try and imagine what the Eucharist is. It is impossible to imagine this presence, it is beyond imagination. But however we try to understand and explain it, we know that it is a unique kind of presence, the real presence of Christ's humanity, a divine presence.

When we are shocked by the mystery and try to find a rational explanation by likening it to other kinds of presence, we are forgetting one thing : the ideas and images that we can form of this reality are bounded by time and space, whereas God is not. The risen Christ himself is not subject to time and space. The real presence in the consecrated bread "breaks into" time and space, it is a sort of window or passage connecting them with eternity. Why? Because this presence gives us a relationship with Jesus as he is now, and also in some way makes Christ's sacrifice on the cross a permanent moment. Jesus died once and for all, and we can investigate the day, the time and the year of his death on Calvary.

Jesus suffered for a few hours, but because he who was suffering and dying was God, the Word of God, his suffering in his human nature, transcended time since God is not in time. So the Eucharist takes us back through the centuries and also transcends time.

Because this sacramental presence is beyond time, when we receive the body of Christ in communion and drink his blood, the temporal distance is done away with and we share mysteriously in his passion, we are really taking part in his Last Supper.

It is also because Jesus is still alive that he can be present in the Eucharist. Jesus is alive in the glory of his risen body. As the apostles saw and felt, he still has the marks of the nails in his hands and feet and the lance wound in his side. His body is outside time and space. He is not in space and so not in the cosmos, not in our universe. He is in a divine universe, where we can also go by faith here on earth, by seeing face-to-face when we die and await the resurrection, and by glory after the resurrection. The Eucharist is a window open on to the world where Jesus is now, risen and alive. That is how the living Jesus is present in a way that transcends space in the consecrated bread. He is present in the manner in which he now exists. We have communion with the living Jesus. It is not merely a memorial of his passion, but a communion with Christ as he is, and that is why the Eucharist is the pledge of resurrection, the seed of glory. This is what St Bonaventure said in a text which the Pope also quoted: "There is no difficulty in Christ being in the sacrament as a sign, but enormous difficulty in his being in the sacrament truly, as he is in heaven." As he is in heaven, if Christ is truly present this can only mean present as he is now. We say "now" because we are in time, but for God, for Christ, there is no past, present or future; it is always "now".

These are just a few reflections on the Eucharist and the presence of Christ's humanity in the sacrament. They are enough to be going on with. We can leave it to the theologians to discuss the manner of this presence; will they ever reach an answer? The mystery cannot be resolved. We must hold fast to what Jesus said, the realism and simplicity of his words, which is also the simplicity of the church's faith, the simplicity of a faith which has taken the words of Jesus as they stand. The early christians took them in this way, so did the apostles and St Paul.

In the end what we must always accept are the words of Jesus. We have the bread of the Eucharist, but it can mean little to us if we do not try to grasp it through the words of Jesus. We can only penetrate the mystery by listening to the Lord. He said: "This is my body, this is my blood of the new covenant." He said that he was giving us his flesh to eat and his blood to drink; that anyone who ate his flesh and drank his blood would have eternal life and be raised up on the last day. That is what we believe.

In conclusion I cannot do better than quote this text from St John: "If a man loves me he will keep my word." We must keep his word. "And my Father will love him, and we will come to him and make our home with him."[21] This is one of the most important sayings for us who long to live with Jesus and see him face-to-face. We know that the Eucharist is given to us as a special meeting place. Where on earth can we meet Christ more completely, meet our saviour who saves and redeems us? What more perfect meeting place than this communion in memory of his passion, in which we

[21] Jn. 14.23.

drink his blood which was shed for the remission of our sins? How better can we prepare for the fulfilment of our hope in our future life and resurrection than by taking into ourselves the body of Christ in his glory, glory which we shall share one day, because we shall be like him when we see him as he is.

We must now go on to consider other aspects of the mystery given to the church, and the manner in which we should receive this gift of Jesus in such a way that we get out of it what he has put into it for each one of us.

The Eucharist Given to the Faith of Believers

We will continue our meditation by thinking of the mystery of the Eucharist as it has been entrusted to the church. Sometimes when we read the gospel we cannot help wishing the Lord had been more explicit about certain things! Without any explanation or comment he did the actions and said the words we have reported and merely added: "Do this in memory of me" . . . We can see how necessary the help of the Holy Spirit was to the church at its beginning, so that first the apostles, then their successors, then all the churches could faithfully repeat and live this mystery in the way Christ wanted. Jesus' own words suggest the depths in it. It is the memorial of the Lord's death, it is also a living and permanent proof of his love, and it is truly "in memory of him" that we celebrate it. The Eucharist is the blood of the covenant which was shed for many for the forgiveness of sins. It is Jesus' flesh and blood, as he himself said, and we must eat and drink it to have eternal life and the promise of resurrection. Isn't it also a promise of closeness to the Lord? Didn't he say that he would dwell in us and we in him, if we ate his flesh and drank his blood?

This mystery has been entrusted to the church. What have we done with it? This is a question each must ask himself. How have I received the mystery in my life, how have I behaved towards it? How do I understand it?

First it demands our faith. It is a mystery of faith. We cannot talk about the Eucharist without talking about faith. The Eucharistic bread and wine are given to us as they appear to our senses. We take part in a liturgy of prayers, rites and ceremonies, which affect our senses, move our hearts and so become graven on our memories. This complex of feelings and habits of mind surrounding and sustaining our faith often also hides its true nature from us. I remember the remark made by a woman who often went to communion and from her childhood had associated all her feelings about the presence of Jesus and closeness to Christ in communion with the sight of the small white wafer. One day she attended a Mass in the Greek rite and said to me: "I can't go to communion any more because I have lost my faith." All she saw at this Mass was ordinary bread, which did not have the same associations for her or evoke the feelings and images she was used to connecting with the round white host. So she thought she had lost her faith! There are also many young people who come to a stage when the violent feelings and imaginings of adolescence go dead on them and they can no longer feel anything during the liturgy. They are bewildered and think they have lost their faith. At this point they need to think about their faith and rediscover it. What they felt before was faith and probably sincere, but not a very enlightened faith. The crisis is an opportunity to come to a more adult faith, a truer faith. We cannot approach the mystery of the Eucharist without faith. In the words of the hymn to the Blessed Sacrament attributed to St Thomas:

Seeing, touching, tasting, all are here deceived;
Nothing but our hearing can safely be believed.
I believe whatever the Son of God has said;
He is Truth and no one can speak a truer word.

This is what faith is. It is nothing to do with feelings or emotions. Of course God may often send us visitations of his spirit to give us feelings of comfort and these are called "consolations". They help us in our weakness. But they are not the basis of our act of faith. The Eucharist demands our faith in the actual bread and wine. And the more the development of the liturgy taking place at the moment in the catholic church upsets our habits, the more we have to rely on naked faith. The bread of the Mass does not look the same; it is baked differently. When Christ the high priest, the one and only priest, has changed this bread and wine into his body and blood by the power of his word, we believe. We believe because of his word, even if we do not feel anything very much. The reforms taking place at the moment are a constant invitation to renew our faith.

In the past nobody touched the Eucharist except the priest. It was kept away from the faithful who only saw it through the incense smoke, in the priest's hands or a golden monstrance surrounded by altar light. All this gave the faithful a feeling of reverence, which was a true feeling. But now we are asked to believe without the support of these solemn and sacred paraphernalia. We have to discover the humbler sign value of ordinary bread and wine, and rediscover through it what Christ did with it. The Eucharist tests our faith, and when our minds accept the words of Jesus alone, as they are reported in the gospel and passed on to us by the church, this is living faith. When we say "Amen" or "I believe" we are truly giving our faith to the presence of Christ in the mystery of the Eucharist.

This mystery has been entrusted to the church. It belongs to the church, Christ's body, so that it may become involved in the sacrifice which Christ its head offered for it.

Because Christ is present in the church and united to it, it is the church which now offers the Eucharistic sacrifice. Thus it becomes the sacrifice of the whole Christ. It is distinct from the sacrifice of the cross, although it is also the same sacrifice. We are united to the ministry of the Eucharist and with the church and with Christ we offer the sacrifice of Christ.

For the Eucharist is first and foremost a sacrifice and that is why it is "at the centre of the liturgy and of all christian life", as Paul VI said in his most recent writings about it. Nothing could be truer, the Eucharist belongs to the church and the church has arranged its whole liturgy round it, because without it the liturgy would have no reason for existing.

The Eucharist is first and foremost a sacrifice. It is the blood of the covenant shed for our many sins, it is the memorial of the Lord's death. We cannot receive with faith the mystery of this sacrifice until we have understood the meaning, for the church and for each one of us, the mystery of Christ's death on the cross. We must understand the reality of the agony in the garden, his sweat of blood, scourging, crowning with thorns, the humiliation of the way of the cross, and the crucifixion and death at the end. All this is in some way contained in the Eucharist. That is why the sacrament is so serious. The Son of Man's sufferings are proof of his love but above all our redemption. Without him we cannot be purified and come to God. Christ offers himself in the Eucharist in a sacrifice of redemption which is also a sacrifice of praise, because Jesus is the glory of the Father and he can now be offered by the church in the name of all men in a perfect sacrifice of praise and thanksgiving.

It is important to remind ourselves here of the meaning of the passover meal during which the Eucharist was instituted. In the history of salvation, and the history of mankind, these few hours of his passion, and in particular the moment when he instituted the Eucharist in the upper room during the passover meal, are unique. It was no ordinary meal. We sometimes forget this. It was not an ordinary meal, it was a passover celebration. We should go back and read what the scriptures tell us about this ritual celebration and what it meant. We should remember the event it celebrated and how all the ceremonies were laid down by Moses under God's own direction.

It celebrated the dramatic exodus from Egypt. The children of Israel were protected by the blood of the lamb they had slain and whose blood they had been told to smear on their doorposts so that the exterminating angel would pass them over. Inside their houses they, with their loins girded, were preparing to set out across the desert for the promised land and escape from their captivity in Egypt. From then on, every year, the celebration of this escape was the climax of Israel's liturgy, it was the climax of the history of their people in its relations with God, the moment when the covenant was solemnly renewed. The lamb to be sacrificed had to be perfect, with no defects, it was to be slaughtered and laid on the firewood. And all these things which happened under the guidance of providence corresponded in God's mind with the vision of Christ the redeemer, crucified, nailed to the wood of the cross, also the lamb without spot. Jesus who celebrated the passover every year with his disciples came to this his last passover knowing that he would be the pascal victim. He knew that the rites prefigured his own sufferings, and that he was the pascal lamb at the centre of the yearly ceremony.

We have read the passage in the scriptures where Jesus says he is anxious for this passover to come but also afraid of it. "I have greatly longed to eat this passover with you before I suffer." Then this passover meal which prefigured his death was fulfilled; during the meal Jesus himself became the bread which had been baked in accordance with the rites celebrating the exodus from Egypt (in their haste they had had no time to bake leavened bread). With the bread and the cup of blessing which was drunk in memory of Israel's liberation and in thanksgiving, Jesus took on his passion. Among his apostles he mysteriously offered his body and blood, the blood of the new covenant which would be sealed a few hours later, and which the Eucharistic passover he now instituted would henceforth recall. This is the reality of the Eucharist, the reality of Christ's sacrifice, the new covenant, the true passover.

The Jews were supposed to prepare themselves body and soul for the yearly celebration of the passover. They read the story of the escape from Egypt to their children so that they would understand the meaning of the celebration they were about to take part in. And how do we prepare for the celebration of the Eucharist, which is a far greater thing than the passover being both sign and reality, whereas the passover was merely the sign and prefiguring symbol? For the blood of the covenant which is given to us is the same blood Christ shed on Calvary.

So we must accept this Eucharist given us by Jesus and share in the priest's offering of the sacrifice. It is necessary for us to offer it because it concerns our redemption.

It is not something outside us which does not really concern us. It is not just a liturgical ceremony but the centre of our christian life. Just because we repeat it every morning or every week, we should not let it go stale on us and lose our reverence for it.

It is not enough to receive it passively. It is not enough merely to take an active part in the singing, the readings and ceremonies which accompany it. This communal participation in the visible sign and its rites must not take the place of a deep and conscious participation in the invisible reality. The sign is meant to lead us somewhere, it is not just a ceremony, its celebration is not just an assembly, because through this sacrament we receive the passion of Christ into our lives. We must freely accept our redemption. God respects our freedom and anything less than a free and loving response to his gift is not enough. He suffered and we in our turn must enter into his sufferings. He saves us and we must let ourselves be saved. The Eucharist requires this faith in our redemption and we must share in this redemption by love and by the cross in our own lives. The Eucharist is the true centre of our lives because it is the mystery of the redemption, it contains the mystery of human rebirth by baptism, the mystery of our christian vocation. That is why we must not only offer the sacrifice with the priest but share in the communion.

We must try and understand more profoundly the meaning of Jesus' words when he said he was the true bread and his flesh was given to us to eat and his blood to drink. I said before that there is a natural continuity in the movement which led the Word to become flesh and Christ to give us the Eucharist. Both are the fulfilment of a single loving intention. We should consider here for a moment how the body and blood of Christ can be a source of grace to us. What is the object of the redemption? Isn't it to restore us to divine sonship? We know that by grace God gives us a share in the divine life and real adoptive sonship, and that this is given to us through the abundant grace in Christ's own humanity. His humanity, body and soul, flesh and blood belongs to the Son of God made man. Jesus is the word made flesh, Son of God by nature. That is why his human nature had the fullest possible share in the divine life, a unique share which was his by right because he was by nature the Father's only Son. In Christ's humanity there was, if I may so put it, an adaption of the divine life to creaturehood, a "humanization" of the divine life, and so Christ is the source whence this life can flood into us. He is the new

Adam. Because Jesus is both Son of God and Son of Man, we in our turn can receive divine adoption from him. It comes from the grace he possesses as head of the body whose members we are.

Jesus' humanity is thus the special instrument of grace. It is a great mystery. We need his humanity to be cured of our weaknesses, purified of our sins and to receive the divine life. In communion we mysteriously eat his humanity. This eating is of a special kind. It is really the body of Christ that we eat, his body as it is now, not in its earthly state, but present in a spiritual, glorious, divine and marvellous way.

Through communion we receive eternal life, as Jesus himself promised. We are doomed to die and we need this assurance of divine life. God alone knows what happens to us after death. We can only wonder what happens when our soul, the principle of human life, is separated from our mortal bodies. It is not easy to believe that this soul is really eternal, we need to know by faith that through Christ's grace our souls are strengthened by the divine life and given the assurance of eternity.

*

We spoke yesterday[22] of the gradual transformation of the christian by the divine love working in him. Our communion in the sacrament of the body and blood of Jesus helps to bring about this transformation. We are not merely united to Christ by faith, we must also be transformed into him by love, love with all its difficulty. We cannot make this transformation ourselves, we can do nothing without Christ's grace and communion in him. So the sacrament of the Eucharist is above all the sacrament of love, and that unity which is the fruit of love. Because the sacrament is entrusted to the church, because it is the sacrament of the church, it is given to us in a liturgical celebration, where christians join in a community of love. The Fathers often pointed out that bread is formed from many grains of wheat and wine is made from many grapes, which is a natural symbol for the unity of the christian people. It is just an image but it has been used again and again to illustrate the church's faith in the Eucharist as the leaven of unity among christians.

*

Here we must say something about the grievous

[22] See note 16.

problem of the division of the churches in the celebration of the Eucharist. We know that as soon as Jesus
had given the sacrament to the church at its beginning,
divisions began to arise within it as to how the mystery
should be understood. The churches had different
beliefs and this lack of unity in faith made intercom-
munion impossible. Of course it is very important to
approach the sacrament with loyalty and sincerity,
because although his presence is real it can have no
effect on us if we do not believe. Christ acts, flesh
profits nothing, the spirit gives life. Our mouths take
the bread, but our hearts and souls must be disposed
by faith to receive Christ as their food, the food of
grace.

The inability to share communion is the strongest
expression of the divisions among christians. It should
distress us greatly and make us very humble. It is not
for us to judge who in the past was responsible for the
disagreement on such an important and sacred subject.

How is it that Jesus' words in their simplicity could
not be understood by everyone in the same way? The
disagreement is so sad. When the Eucharist one day
reunites all christians in one communion, it will reach
its fulness as a sign of unity. It is the sign of unity
because we cannot rest while there are divisions over it.
We cannot come to the body of Christ without feeling

the pain of not being able to share in it all together, because our faith is not yet perfectly united. Christ expects this unity from us.

*

I must now talk about one last aspect of the Eucharist; it is the sacrament which brings us close to God. Jesus said that those who ate his flesh and drank his blood would dwell in him and he in them. He spoke of this closeness on another occasion : "If a man loves me, he will keep my word, and my father will love him, and we will come to him, and make our home with him."[23]

Yes, we are God's dwelling place. God dwells in us and we in God. What does this mean? It means a relationship between persons because we are persons, Jesus is a person and our God is the God of the living. So it can only mean an exchange of knowledge and love, because these are what define human life and we know that we are made in God's image and he is supreme knowledge and love. So these must be the basis of any relationship with God. As it says in the encyclical of Paul VI I have already quoted[24] : "We must not think

[23] Cf. note 21.
[24] *Mysterium Fidei.*

of spiritual union with Christ, which is the purpose of this sacrament, as lasting only as long as the ceremony of the Eucharist. Obviously our spiritual union with Christ is not merely momentary." Of course we have a very special kind of communion with Christ at the moment when we receive him in the sacrament, because in a mysterious way we truly take into ourselves his body and blood. But the result of receiving his body and blood is that God dwells in us more fully and we in him. This dwelling in one another brings a closeness which should continue and increase. It is measured by the strength of our faith and of our charity. The goal of this closeness is the vision of God, nothing less, in the fulness of glory after the resurrection. This is the goal but it must begin here on earth. This closeness to God which is the fruit of the sacrament of the Eucharist depends on our personal response, our collaboration, because it means knowing and loving, it involves our minds and hearts, faith and charity, the contemplation of God and his love. Our whole being is involved in this relationship in which everything comes from us and at the same time everything comes from God. This is why it is so important to come to the liturgy of the Eucharist knowing what it is about, close personal union with Christ.

We should also say something about the long and

silent contemplation of the mystery of the Eucharist which should go on outside the Mass itself. Of course the first question to ask here is this : does the humanity of Christ remain present in the sacrament after the Mass is ended ?

Our faith – I mean here the faith of the catholic church – firmly accepts that his presence remains, according to the constant tradition of the catholic church. I am not speaking of any particular form that devotion to the Blessed Sacrament may have taken in the past. The forms have been different at different times. I mean simply faith in the permanence of Christ's presence in the sacrament after the Mass, even when this presence had no particular cult attached to it. We believe that this presence is real and permanent because it is the work of Christ himself. A presence brought about by the power of Christ is not suddenly going to stop at some arbitrary moment. Christ would have to intervene again, if I may so put it. The purpose of this presence is communion and that is why it does not end when the communicant has digested the consecrated bread. From the beginning it was customary in the church to set aside some of the bread used in the Mass, so that it could be taken to martyrs in prison and to the sick and the dying.

We believe in Christ's enduring presence in the con-

secrated bread and wine, when they have been con-
sumed in communion. Once we have established this,
how can we blame the believer for feeling the need to
adore this mysterious presence which is divine? How
can we blame him for seeking from this presence comfort in his prayers and strength in his temptations? Why
should the action of the sacrament be confined within
the Mass, during which we sometimes do not have
leisure and peace enough to open our hearts in faith
and love and longing for our God? Meditation on such
a great mystery needs silence and a long time spent in
prayer. And should not this union with Christ which is
the purpose of the sacrament in the liturgy be developed
and deepened in a free and loving way in our own
lives? Shouldn't each one of us have a personal life
of contemplation and love for Christ? We know that
this is how we should contemplate the Father because
he has revealed himself to us in Jesus, and because
we have received the Holy Spirit from him who gives
us some of his light inaccessible to make us able to know
and love him better.

*

Here let me tell you about our own lives, I mean the
lives of the Little Brothers and Little Sisters, of our

personal experience in following the man of God[25] who
withdrew into the desert and was transformed into a
high degree of likeness to Christ by the purity of his
love and by his deep and close union with Christ. This
union grew closer and closer not only through meditating on the scriptures and taking part in the Eucharistic sacrifice, but also by long and silent adoration of
the Blessed Sacrament.

Some kinds of grace God gives only in silence and
solitary conversation with him. This is a way of giving
himself to us which cannot happen amid noise and
crowds or even in the christian assembly, come together in Christ's name. We have to acknowledge all
sides of human nature. Man is a social being who
needs other people for his mind and heart to be able to
act and grow. This social dimension is part of his
nature. But privacy is also essential to him. This privacy
has certain requirements; friendship and love do not
develop easily without private conversation. This is also
part of human nature. Our ideas of human nature are
often influenced by our conception of our final
destiny? What then is this final destiny? If we believe
that, as Jesus promised, we shall one day rise with him,
and that as full human beings and sons of God

---

[25] Charles de Foucauld, whose life and spirituality provide the
inspiration for the Little Brothers and Little Sisters.

we shall reach a state of love we cannot imagine here below, because we shall be united to the source of love, then I find it easier to understand my destiny as a person and all that this entails in life here on earth. The Eucharist reaches the personal core of each one of us. Of course we are members of one another in Christ's body, we are a christian assembly, we are the people of God, because we need a community to reach our final personal goal. But it is not enough for us to be no more than part of a whole, even if that whole is the body of the church. We need also to know that we are persons, absolutely unique and made in God's image.

But do we know what a person is? This is a mystery which each of us possesses and never fully understands. Each of us is his own centre and distinct from his brother. There have been generations before us and after our death generations will follow us. Each of us will have lived at a particular moment of time, in a particular space, and each is the centre of his own being, with God and in him.

How else can we understand the great love of the saints, Mary Magdalene's passionate attachment to the Lord? We cannot live without him. If this is our final end, then it must begin here below. If I love the Lord, how can I not worship his mystery in the sacrament, how can I not overflow with love and reverence for this wonder that Christ has worked in his love for me? How can I not adore his presence when I know it is real? I think there is a danger at the moment of too strong a reaction, as often happens, against the abuses of too individualistic and unliturgical a piety. I think the danger is now that piety might become too communal and liturgical. The reaction may go too far and threaten christians' personal life, causing them to forget that liturgy cannot be separated from private prayer, that by our private relationship of faith and love alone with Christ, we both prepare for the liturgy and profit from it.

And we must also not forget that there are other sorts of divine presence in our lives besides the one we have been speaking of. In particular we should remember God's presence by grace in those he has redeemed. This presence of the Trinity deep within us is a presence we can neither feel nor consciously apprehend, because it is an object of faith. We believe that we have become God's children by baptism and have received the grace of adoption. We believe that we have a share in the divine life. We have no conscious awareness of it. We cannot prove God's presence by experience, we believe in it. Just as the Lord's presence in the Eucharist is beyond all physical experience and rational proof, just as even our inmost senses cannot feel the body of Christ we receive in communion, so the grace of divine life in us, the seed of eternal life, our sharing in the close union of the three persons of the Trinity, is beyond experience. But this is how God dwells in us. He is not outside us but very near – within our deepest being. We are impoverished and may lose our way towards our final destination if we forget that what we have to seek lies within ourselves and nowhere else. Seeking God in our neighbour is a different thing. We can admire God's work in our brothers, we can admire the wonders of his grace. Neither am I forgetting that when we love the least of our brethren we are loving Christ himself. But God's own life in our deepest self is something quite other; it is the beginning of our rebirth into the life of glory. Because of this divine presence in us men have buried themselves in the desert seeking solitude. Because of this divine presence every christian needs a minimum of private personal prayer, otherwise he may no longer understand what he is as a human being and a son of God.

I have tried, far from adequately, to remind you of the Lord's teaching on the Eucharist. We have Jesus' own words, we can only take them to heart and try to assimilate them. We must hope that the Holy Spirit will help us come to their true meaning. We are poor and ignorant but we can take comfort from Jesus saying to his apostles shortly before he left them, that they could not understand all that he had taught them, and it was good for him to go away so that he could send the Spirit to them, and this Spirit would lead them to understand the things they had been told. "But the Counsellor, the Holy Spirit, whom the Father will send in my name, he will teach you all things, and bring to your remembrance all that I have said to you. When the Spirit of truth comes, he will guide you into all truth"[26] And surely we must long to understand better and better this great mystery of the Eucharist which Christ gave us in his love.

And let us not forget that Jesus himself said that only childlike faith can be sufficiently enlightened by the grace of the Holy Spirit to understand this mystery of the Eucharist the better to live from it. Let us try to win the Lord's admiration which led him to cry: "I thank thee Father, Lord of heaven and earth, that thou hast hidden these things from the wise and understanding and revealed them to babes."[27]

Perhaps all the disputes and disagreements about the Eucharist were caused by men wanting to be too wise and understanding. We shall only regain the unity of faith if we become capable of fully receiving God's revelation promised to little ones.

[26] Jn. 14.26; 16.13.   [27] Lk. 10.21.

PETALS OF PRAYER: Creative Ways To Pray

By Rev. Paul Sauvé 1.50

"Petals of Prayer *is an extremely practical book for anyone who desires to pray but has difficulty finding a method for so doing. At least 15 different methods of prayer are described and illustrated in simple, straightforward ways, showing they can be contemporary even though many of them enjoy a tradition of hundreds of years. In an excellent introductory chapter, Fr. Sauvé states that the best 'method' of prayer is the one which unites us to God. . . . Father Sauvé masterfully shows how traditional methods of prayer can be very much in tune with a renewed church."*
St. Anthony Messenger

CRISIS OF FAITH
Invitation to Christian Maturity 1.50

By Rev. Thomas Keating, ocso. How to hear ourselves called to discipleship in the Gospels is Abbot Thomas' important and engrossing message. As Our Lord forms His disciples, and deals with His friends or with those who come asking for help in the Gospels, we can receive insights into the way He is forming or dealing with us in our day to day lives.

IN GOD'S PROVIDENCE:
The Birth of a Catholic
Charismatic Parish 1.50

By Rev. John Randall. The engrossing story of the now well-known Word of God Prayer Community in St. Patrick's Parish, Providence, R.I. as it developed from Father Randall's first adverse reaction to the budding Charismatic Movement to today as it copes with the problems of being a truly pioneer Catholic Charismatic Parish.

"This splendid little volume bubbles over with joy and peace, with 'Spirit' and work."
The Priest

SOURCE OF LIFE:
The Eucharist and Christian Living 1.50

By Rev. Rene Voillaume. A powerful testimony to the vital part the Eucharist plays in the life of a Christian. It is a product of a man for whom Christ in the Eucharist is nothing less than all.

**Order from your bookstore or
LIVING FLAME PRESS, Locust Valley, N.Y. 11560**

SEEKING PURITY OF HEART:
THE GIFT OF OURSELVES TO GOD
illus 1.25

By Joseph Breault. For those of us who feel that we do not live up to God's calling, that we have sin of whatever shade within our hearts. This book shows how we can begin a journey which will lead from our personal darkness to wholeness in Christ's light — a purity of heart. Clear, practical help is given us in the constant struggle to free ourselves from the deceptions that sin has planted along all avenues of our lives.

PROMPTED BY THE SPIRIT
2.25

By Rev. Paul Sauvé. A handbook by a Catholic Charismatic Renewal national leader for all seriously concerned about the future of the renewal and interested in finding answers to some of the problems that have surfaced in small or large prayer groups. It is a call to all Christians to find answers with the help of a wise Church tradition as transmitted by her ordained ministers. The author has also written *Petals of Prayer/Creative Ways to Pray.*

DISCOVERING PATHWAYS TO PRAYER
1.75

By Msgr. David E. Rosage. Following Jesus was never meant to be dull, or worse, just duty-filled. Those who would aspire to a life of prayer and those who have already begun, will find this book amazingly thorough in its scripture-punctuated approach.

"A simple but profound book which explains the many ways and forms of prayer by which the person hungering for closer union with God may find him." **Emmanuel Spillane, O.C.S.O., Abbot, Our Lady of the Holy Trinity Abbey, Huntsville, Utah.**

THE BOOK OF REVELATION:
What Does It Really Say?
1.75

By Rev. John Randall S.T.D. The most discussed book of the Bible today is examined by a scripture expert in relation to much that has been published and the Truth. A simply written and revealing presentation.

Order from your bookstore or
LIVING FLAME PRESS, Locust Valley, N.Y. 11560

LIVING FLAME PRESS
BOX 74
LOCUST VALLEY, N.Y. 11560

Order from your bookstore or use this coupon.

Please send me:

Quantity

_____	**Source of Life — $1.50**
_____	**The Book of Revelation — $1.75**
_____	**Reasons for Rejoicing — $1.75**
_____	**Discovering Pathways to Prayer — $1.75**
_____	**Prompted by the Spirit — $2.25**
_____	**Prayer of Love — $1.50**
_____	**Prayer, Aspiration & Contemplation — $3.95**
_____	**Union with the Lord — $.85**
_____	**Enfolded by Christ — $1.95**
_____	**Contemplative Prayer — $1.75**
_____	**Attaining Spiritual Maturity — $.85**
_____	**Petals of Prayer — $1.50**
_____	**Seeking Purity of Heart — $1.25**
_____	**Crisis of Faith — $1.50**
_____	**In God's Providence — $1.50**
_____	**The One Who Listens — $2.25**

QUANTITY ORDER: DISCOUNT RATES

For convents, prayer groups, etc.: $10 to $25 = 10%;
$26 to $50 = 15%; over $50 = 20%.
Booksellers: 40%, 30 days net.

NAME_____

ADDRESS_____

CITY_____ STATE _____ ZIP _____

☐ *Payment enclosed. Kindly include $.35 postage and handling on
order up to $5.00. Above that, include 5% of total. Thank you.*